# REPTILES

## Laurence Perkins

Octopus Books

# Contents

# Introduction

The term 'reptile' is used generally to describe the group of creeping or crawling vertebrate creatures which includes snakes, lizards, crocodiles, turtles and tortoises. It also embraces the group called amphibians which includes frogs, toads, newts and salamanders, whose young have gills like fishes. Many reptiles, like crocodiles, could be said to be 'amphibious' since this term also means that they live both on land and in water. However, the frogs, toads, newts and salamanders are distinct in that they have to return to water to lay their eggs.

The thought of crocodiles, snakes and toads does not appeal to many people but it is a great pity that dislike of these creatures often leads them to dismiss all the reptiles outright, without realizing how greatly they vary in every way and how attractive some species are. The tiny sunloving lizards with wizened faces, the multi-coloured chameleons, the intelligent tortoises and impressive turtles are all thoroughly acceptable creatures. Other reptiles have fascinating patterns of behaviour and special adaptions suited to their particular life style. The tendency to dislike reptiles and amphibians on sight probably stemmed from their habit of sleeping in secluded places where one stumbles on them, frightening both oneself and the creature. It has also been fostered by religious teachings which have emphasized the idea that serpents and toads are the forms inhabited by evil spirits.

Reviewing reptiles and amphibians without prejudice, it is important to say first of all that they are not, as commonly supposed, slimy and repulsive to the touch. Amphibians are damp but not slimy (in other words, they are not covered with mucus as are fish). Reptiles are scaley or plated, quite dry to the touch and perhaps silky in the case of many small-scaled snakes and lizards. Most of them are harmless, some are venomous but nearly all are retiring and unlikely to attack unless provoked, with the possible exception of some of the crocodiles and the big monitors.

All reptiles evolved from amphibians during the carboniferous period more than 200 million years ago. Amphibians were the first creatures to emerge from the sea and to develop lungs to enable them to breath upon land. Over millions of years the true reptiles evolved from those species which became more and more terrestrial and less dependant upon water. Prevailing conditions favoured their development and reptiles prospered as the dominant life-form over a period of 130 million years or more. Although many of them assumed only modest proportions, others were colossal and are known from fossil findings to have reached lengths of 30 to 35 metres and weights of 40 tons or more. With climatic changes and extreme variations in temperature, these monsters eventually perished. The smaller reptiles survived because of their ability to creep into holes and other retreats which offered them protection from severely low temperatures.

The 'age of reptiles' ended more than 100 million years ago,

as the evolution of mammals which has culminated in man progressed. The smaller reptiles continued to adapt to changing conditions and have successfully survived throughout the world except in regions of extreme cold.

As with so many other wild creatures, the security of many reptiles and amphibians is threatened as man takes over more and more undeveloped territory for his own use. Until quite recently this fact had made no impact upon the majority of people who are either antipathetic or apathetic in their attitude towards reptiles. However, with the formation of world organizations concerned with preservation and conservation and through television programmes and numerous films, the need to protect all forms of wild life is becoming much more widely recognized.

RIGHT *Forest Tree Frog*
BELOW *Chameleo Dilepis*

# Frogs and toads

Of all the reptiles and amphibians the frogs and toads are the most well known and practically everybody has collected frog spawn and tadpoles as a child, or come face to face with a frog or toad at some stage. There is not a great deal to distinguish the two. The frogs differ from the toads mainly in the structure of the shoulder girdle with the solitary exception of a small group, the Anglossa, whose members are also tongueless. Often toads have the distinction of warty or granulated skins. This difference, however, cannot be relied upon with all species to determine whether they are frogs or toads. The familiar European tree frog, *Hyla arborea,* has a smooth skin but is, in fact, a toad, while the African clawed toad, *Xenopus laevis*, is a frog. Very small anatomical differences decide whether certain genera are frogs or toads. In spite of this, however, toads can generally be recognized by their dryer, warty skin and by the way they shamble around, making short hops. The common frog, by comparison, has a moist, smooth skin and executes long hops.

Many species of toads are not so agile as the frogs and shamble around making short hops unlike a frog's great leaps. Apart from the tree 'frogs' which seek their food among the foliage of shrubs and small trees, toads are more terrestrial than frogs, although they also must avoid getting too dry and make occasional visits to water. Frogs, on the other hand, rarely wander far from water except in rainy weather or after a heavy dew, preferring to remain in or beside it. Water attracts many insects, of course, such as mayflies, dragonflies, gnats and mosquitos which are a frog's main food supply. After dark, frogs will hunt for prey on land, such as slugs, worms, earwigs and beetles. Toads, too, are mainly nocturnal feeders, spending the daylight hours holed up in a cool, but not too dry, niche.

Among the more impressive frogs is the American Bullfrog, *Rana catesbeiana* which is large enough to tackle things like fish, voles, small snakes and young water fowl. Like many tropical and European species it can make a surprisingly loud noise, the result of special vocal sacs, one on each side of the head, which it can inflate to produce a penetrating croak. Their croaking choruses in the breeding season can be heard a mile or more away. The laughing frog, *R, ridibunda*, is the nearest relative to the American Bullfrog in Europe. Long after the common frog has ceased to croak at the close of the mating season in April, the laughing frog, which breeds some time afterwards, continues to croak throughout the summer and will break into song at any opportunity – even the passing of a car or an aeroplane.

The European midwife toad, *Alytes obstetricans*, has the peculiar habit of collecting the typical toad spawn string as the female expels it and winding it around himself. He then carries the eggs around with him wherever he goes for two or three weeks until they are ready to hatch when he disentangles himself from the eggs and leaves them in the water to hatch. It would seem that this mobility of the small number of eggs laid is the result of an involuntary protective reaction, reducing their time in the water and thus their chance of being attacked by egg-eating fish. This toad is also called the bell toad because of its feeble song which resembles the sound of a tiny bell.

Frogs and toads don't have the keen sense of smell of the salamanders and rely entirely on their sharp eye sight to catch their food. Toads appear to deliberate for some time before flicking out their sticky tongues to trap their prey. Frogs are quicker to respond and some species are very adept at catching insects, even such swift fliers as dragonflies, on the wing.

Toads are credited with a higher I.Q. than frogs since there are a number of recorded accounts of their apparent intelligent behaviour. There are stories of them squatting on the steps of a beehive, nimbly catching the bees as they emerge; and others of their taking up a station at night beneath a scarecrow in order to catch the earwigs that drop from their daytime hideouts in the folds of the dummy's clothing. It is evident that toads will quickly learn to recognize a food source and come to it.

With their great agility, frogs instinctively fly in the face of threatened danger whereas the more lethargic toads rely on quite a different ruse. Adopting what is known as the defence attitude, the toad stretches its hind legs, lifts its behind and lowers its head to the ground while inflating its lungs to increase its size by approximately 50 per cent. It is thought that the increase in size is intended to confuse an attacking snake which, conscious of its limitations, is deterred from tackling what now seems a larger mouthful than before.

The mating of frogs and toads involves the endearing act of amplexus in which the male tightly cuddles the female until she expels her eggs. After the male has fertilized them the male and female each go their own way and the male may well mate several times.

In the choice of spawning sites, many species of toads, and *Bufo bufo* in particular, are far more selective than frogs. Within a certain area, such toads will favour one particular pond in which to foregather each year and reject all other seemingly suitable ponds. Taken away in the breeding season and introduced, for instance, to one's garden pond nearby, a coupled pair will almost certainly leave their new quarters and with the little male riding pick-a-back on the female return to their chosen pond.

# True frogs

**Common European frog** *Rana temporaria*.
At one time this was truly the common
frog of Europe but many different forms of
pollution have greatly reduced its numbers,
especially in parts of Britain. This is a frog
of the temperate zones but it has been found
as far north as the fringe of the Arctic
Circle. It is one of the most innocuous of
of all the frogs. Its voice, which is a very
subdued croak, is heard only during the
short breeding season. Most of the insects
and other creatures that it eats are pests and
it deserves to be regarded as beneficial to
men. Unfortunately many thousands of
common frogs are sacrificed on dissecting
tables in the instruction of embryo biolo-
gists.

RIGHT
**Common frogs** *Rana temporaria* At the onset
of winter, frogs go down to the mud at
the bottom of ponds and hibernate. Although odd spells of mild weather during
the winter may bring them to the surface, it
is not until mid-February that they appear
in numbers around the pondside. They grow
more active as the breeding season ap-
proaches and males and females begin to pair
off. The males croak to attract the females
and clasp their chosen partner in a tight hug
preparatory to spawning and fertilization.

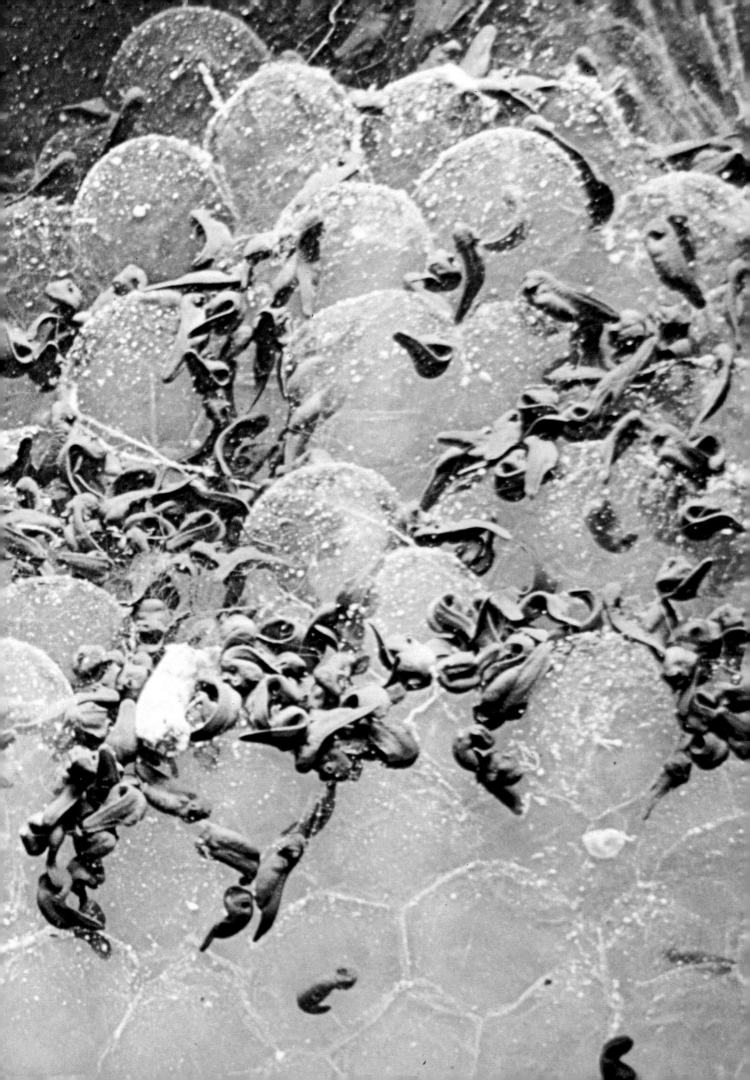

PREVIOUS PAGE
**Common frog tadpoles.** When frog spawn is first deposited it is in a tight mass the size of a golf-ball. It swells rapidly in volume to the size of a coconut and floats on the water surface. The nuclei of the eggs subdivide and the embryos form. The tiny tadpoles then emerge and feed upon the jelly as shown in the photograph, until they free themselves and swim. They then feed on the algal growth on the leaves of aquatic plants.

LEFT
**The edible frog** *Rana esculenta* is the frog whose hind legs are considered a delicacy, particularly by the French. It is found in Europe, and, although it has been introduced into Britain it does not seem to prosper. It is a true water lover, and although it enjoys sunbathing, it rarely strays far from the water side. Its croaking is very loud during the breeding season, and is produced with the aid of two vocal sacs, one on each side of the head. This is a much more agile and colourful creature than the common frog, with longer and more powerful hind legs, and richer markings on the streamlined head.

BELOW
**Laughing frog** *Rana ridibunda*. Another species from Europe, this frog is in many ways similar to the edible frog but grows to a larger size. Known in Britain as the marsh frog, it colonized much of the Romney Marshes where a small number were released in 1935. They thrived in the area with its intersecting ditches and dykes, and

their numbers grew until now they cover more than 100 square miles. In the breeding season their loud laughing croak fills the air between the hours of daylight and darkness. They feed on insects, tadpoles, newts, other frogs, fish and small mammals and have been seen to try and catch a swooping swallow.

RIGHT

**The bull frog** *Rana catesbeiana* is the largest species of North American frogs, reaching a length of 20 cms. Indigenous to the United States east of the Rocky Mountains and also to northern Mexico, it has been introduced to Canada, Cuba and Hawaii. Very aquatic, bull frogs are not often found out of the water where they prey upon crayfish, other frogs, fish, aquatic insects such as dragonflies, small water snakes and even young alligators. In the larval form, the bull frog succumbs to a number of predators and only a fraction of the 10 to 20,000 eggs laid by a female reach maturity.

BELOW

**Leopard frog** *Rana pipiens*. More commonly known in its native North America as the meadow frog, *R. pipiens* is rarely far from water. When disturbed, it gains sanctuary in water by executing a single leap. Experiments have shown its sight to be more sensitive to the blue region of the spectrum and the conclusion is that water reflects the more usual blue of the sky. The leopard frog is, thus, impelled to jump towards a blue area rather than a green one.

# True toads

**Green toad** *Bufo viridis*. Although found in parts of Western Europe, the habitat of this toad spread from Sweden to North Africa and parts of Asia. Attractively marked with patches of green which give it its common name, *B.viridis* is often found in brackish water. The male has a particularly large vocal sac which produces a sustained trilling croak. Mating takes place during April and May when two strings of spawn comprising 10 to 20 thousand eggs are laid.

**Common toad** *Bufo bufo*. Toads may occupy the same territory (one's garden, for example) for many years and they also become attached to particular hunting grounds and favourite retreats within that territory. They rarely return to water after the breeding season as their skins do not dry up as much as those of frogs. They seek food mostly after dark and spend much of the day shielded from the glare of the sun in holes where it is cool and damp. The photograph shows a toad in a cave on a rockery which it has used for nearly ten years.

**Natterjack toad** *Bufo calamita*. Found throughout Europe and in a few places in Britain, this is a smaller species than the common toad and runs rather than hops. The dorsal stripe, shown in the photograph, is another of its distinguishing characteristics. It likes sandy soil and brackish water for spawning, and has the loudest croak of all European toads. It deposits its spawn in twin strings, like the green toad, and not in a single strand as does the common toad.

# Tree frogs

LEFT
**American green tree frog** *Hyla cinerea*. This species is common in the Florida Everglades and its territory extends westwards to Texas. Like its European congener, *H. arborea*, it displays great versatility in colour-changing technique, assuming a garb of grey during cool weather when it becomes less active and becoming yellow when croaking repeatedly. It is said to 'sing' more readily during rainy weather, and is regarded locally as a weather forecaster.

BELOW LEFT
**European tree frog** *Hyla arborea*. This little leaf-green frog is commonly found in central Europe on bramble bushes. There it blends perfectly with the foliage, basks contentedly in the sunshine feeding upon insects visiting the flowers and fruit. It returns to water in the breeding season, and its spawn clusters undergo the usual metamorphosis. The adhesive discs on all four feet give this climber a firm grip on the smoothest and most vertical of surfaces and they have been known to climb something like a glossy-tiled wall with alacrity. Depending on the intensity of the sunlight and the colour of its surroundings, this tree frog can change colour quite dramatically to a pale grey or brown. The photograph shows a tree frog on apple blossom.

RIGHT

**Barking tree frog** *Hyla gratiosa*. Although it is only seven cms in length, this is the largest of the North American tree frogs. Most of its kind are very vocal with croaks in the higher register but this species has a deep bark produced by its large vocal sac which gives it its name. This frog can swing in true trapeze fashion from one leaf to another balancing lightly and rapidly on a single toe.

ABOVE

**The forest tree frog** *Leptopelis natalensis* is a secretive species of the Rhacophoridae famil from the forests of the east coast of Southern Africa. The large pupils of the eyes are especially noteworthy. The enlarged 'finger' tips are well-displayed in the photographs. Tree frogs, like other frogs, cast or slough their skins, but where as this is an occasional exercise with most frogs, many of the tree frogs perform this operation every night.

RIGHT

**Gliding frog** *Rhacophorus spp*. Gliding frogs are members of a family of tree frogs found in Borneo and Malaya. They mate in trees overhanging the water, and when the female lays the eggs she also excretes albumen to make a foam nest. Both sexes can be seen whisking it into a froth with their hind legs. The outside of the nest forms a crust while the inside remains sufficiently liquid for the eggs to float in it. When the crust ruptures, the eggs or tadpoles drop into the water below. Like other tree frogs, their toes terminate in sucker discs for clinging to trees.

LEFT

**Spring peeper** *Hyla crucifer*. The specific name of this little tree frog refers to the 'X' marking on its back. A North American species, it is one of the harbingers of spring. Its voice, in chorus with many others, carries over long distances and is likened to the sound of bells. Spending more of its time in the water than in the trees, the spring peeper has less well-developed toe-discs than most of the other tree frogs but is still able to climb among the branches, leaping from one to another with great agility and covering many times its own length with each leap.

LEFT

**Cricket frog** *Acris crepitans*. Only three and a half cms long, this frog's jump has been calculated as thirty-six times its own length. It has a high-pitched, clicking call which carries for long distances and cricket frogs have been known to call throughout the winter months. The eggs are laid early in spring and metamorphose from May to October. Many of the tiny froglets fall victim to a host of fish, bird and reptile predators. The skin is very warty and granulated.

BELOW

**The Cuban tree frog** *Hyla septentrionalis* is the largest species of the genus and an average specimen measures around 13 cms in length. Native to Cuba and the Bahamas, it can now be found in Florida where its introduction has prospered. It has a loud, harsh call and, being of a solitary disposition, sings solo rather than in chorus. It shows little fear of man, which may explain why so many of these frogs get loaded on to ships along with fruit cargoes and have thus extended their territories.

# Reed frogs and others

ABOVE
**The green reed frog** *Hyperolius tuberilinguis*
is a rare species from the east coast of
Africa south of the equator. There is no
patterning at all on the brilliant green back
which contrasts with the white belly,
although the hind legs are relieved with
some pink. The eyes are exceptionally large.
During the breeding season the male reed
frog sings by inflating and deflating his
large throat pouch containing special vocal
chords.

FOLLOWING PAGE
**The painted reed frog** *Hyperolius marmoratus*
is found from the eastern parts of southern
Africa through to Malawi and is one of
200 species which live in Africa. It is
approximately $2\frac{1}{2}$ cms in length. The colour
pattern, which ranges from black and
yellow, brown and yellow and black, red
and yellow, varies with each specimen and
changes in response to stimuli from temperature and background. These frogs cling
to the reed stems and bask in the sun while
awaiting the passing of flying insects. When
disturbed, they drop quickly into the water.

PAGE 21
**Corroboree frog** *Pseudophryne corroboree*.
This 'false toad' from Australia belongs to
the large family Leptodactylidae which
includes some of the world's most colourful
frogs. Leptodactylids abound in South
America and Australia. Those of the genus
*Pseudophryne* lay their eggs in a damp place
under stones, selecting a time when rainfall
is heavy enough to soak the ground. Rain
can fall at any time within a six month
period and this accomodating species fits in
with the weather. The distinctive colouring
is a warning to predators.

LEFT
**The running frog** *Kassina senegalensis* is a
nocturnal member of a group of striped
frogs from Africa, and measures 8
cms in length. Its vocal accomplishments are
reminiscent of the popping sound of a
cork. It frequents open grassland extending
from the Sahara to the Cape and its colouring camouflages it well although it does not
risk daylight appearances. It runs in similar
fashion to the natterjack toad instead of
hopping like other frogs.

BELOW LEFT
**Water Lily frog** *Hyperolius pusillus*. The
African genus *Hyperolius* embraces more
than 200 species of so-called reed frogs
which display a very wide range of patterns
and colours. Most of them have bizarre
colour combinations, although a few are
one colour all over. One, the arum frog,
*H. horstockii,* is of great brilliance, being
ivory white and is inconspicuous in the
arum lily flower which is one of its favourite
haunts. The photograph shows how well
the water lily frog's colouring merges with
that of the water lily pads.

RIGHT
**Chiromantis xerampolina** Another member
of the family Rhacophoridae is seen
here with a large foam nest hanging from a
tree above the water. Although the name
paradoxical frog has been applied to quite a
different species, *C. xerampolina* is equally
deserving of the title because, unlike most
frogs which welcome the rain, this species
goes out of its way to avoid the wet. Its toes
are opposable so that it can get a good grip
upon upright stems without having to rely
totally upon the suction discs.

BELOW
**Wallace's flying frog** *Rhacophorus
nigropalmatus*. This is one of the numerous
Rhacophorid species and comes from
Malaya. The common name stems from its
perfection of the gliding technique and from
Alfred Russell Wallace, who first submitted
details of its behaviour to Europe. Wallace's
reports were disbelieved until confirmed
years later. The enlarged webs of all four
feet are used to obtain air buoyancy and the
belly assumes a concave curve. Experiments,
conducted with Tree Frogs with greatly
reduced webbing, show that when dropped
from forty metres they land gently at a
point twenty seven metres directly beneath
the spot from which they were dropped.

# Newts and salamanders

The amphibians are usually regarded as an intermediate group falling between fishes and reptiles. They emerge from the eggs that have been laid in water as tadpoles with gills and, with a few exceptions, undergo a change, as their limbs appear, from gill-breathing to lung-breathing. Some leave the water when fully metamorphosed (or fully developed), only returning to breed and deposit their eggs; while others divide their time between the two habitats, like many of the frogs and toads.

Amphibians have soft skins through which they are able to increase their intake of oxygen. (Reptiles, on the other hand, have hard, protective coverings.) Their skin has to be consistently damp for them to benefit from this extra means of respiration which is why they avoid direct sunlight and stay in damp, cool places.

Sometimes amphibians fail to undergo complete metamorphosis. Their sexual organs fail to develop and the animal remains immature. This Peter Pan-like phenomenon is known as 'partial neotony' and happens occasionally among frogs and toads as well as newts and salamanders. Some of the newts and salamanders, however, remain in the larval state permanently. This is known as total neotony. The result is normal growth and normal ability to reproduce but the gills are retained instead of being replaced by lungs. The Mexican Axolotl is the best known example of this phenomenon.

Amphibians periodically cast their skins. Newts, wriggling free of their old skin will leave it floating in its entirety upon the water surface or entangled among the water plants. If you find one of these fragile skins complete you can carefully spread it on a flat surface and see the shape of the newt from the tip of each toe to the extreme end of the tail. Frogs and toads who cast their skin less easily than the newts, rid themselves of it piecemeal and then eat it.

Amphibians are divided into three orders: the Gymnophiona (the legless blindworms); the Caudata (the newts and salamanders) and the Salientia (the tailless frogs and toads). The limbless blindworms hail from the tropical regions of America, Africa and Asia and burrow in the soil in search of insect grubs and worms. Newts and salamanders are found in a variety of forms throughout the temperate zones of the world and include many species familiar to children, such as the European crested newt and the Axolotl. The distinction between newts and salamanders is scientifically non-existent; they all belong to the family Salamandridae. The three species indigenous to Britain are referred to as newts, and the name is a corruption of the Anglo-Saxon word 'efete' or 'evete'

which became 'ewt'. The name travelled to America with English settlers and remains in use there though in a wider sense.

During courtship male salamanders either turn darker in colour or raise a crest the length of their backs and sometimes the two display features are combined. The display attracts any female who has not already paired off and fertilization occurs internally. The females lay their eggs singly, several months later in the case of some species and carefully wrap each egg in an underwater plant leaf with their hindlegs before leaving them.

In the initial stages of development the tadpoles do not differ superficially from those of frogs and toads. The forelegs of salamander tadpoles develop before the hind legs, whereas with the frogs and toads the hindlegs precede the forelegs, probably because of the greater length and strength the hindlegs will eventually attain.

Many of the salamanders have the ability to replace any limbs they lose and can re-grow feet, legs and their tail when necessary. These powers of regeneration slacken off with age and may be accomplished only in part. Although salamanders possess a larynx, they are not capable of producing much more than a squeak. As one might imagine their squeaks do not play any part in the pairing of the sexes in the breeding season, as do the nuptial croakings of the frogs and toads. However, their senses of sight and smell are very keenly developed and both are essential to them in finding and catching their prey, although they rely most on their keen eyesight.

Salamanders are able to live for many years and warty newts have lived for up to 25 years in captivity. They are unlikely to live for so long in the wild since they have a large number of enemies: fish, dragon-fly larvae, water-beetles and water fowl in the water, and snakes, rats, hedgehogs and weasels on land.

Salamanders usually hibernate on land, leaving the water in late autumn and crawling under stones or logs and into holes and crevices. They can often be found sandwiched into such small spaces between flat surfaces, like pieces of slate, that it is hard to believe that they can still be alive. Mild periods during the winter will sometimes induce them to re-enter the water, probably in search of food. With the coming of spring, mature salamanders emerge from hibernation and take to the water. The younger ones continue to live on land for up to two years, until sufficiently mature to join the adults in the water during the spring.

**The common or smooth newt** *Triturus vulgaris* is a popular aquarium pet with children. During May and June many ponds teem with smooth newts preparing to breed. The females heavily outnumber the males which carry a crest along the length of the tail during this time. The skin is very smooth and feels slimy when the creature is wet but when he is dry on land his skin is finely granulated and has a matt surface. The young lose their gills and quit the water in early autumn, and can often be found squeezed together in small crevices under stones at the pond's edge.

The illustration, centre right, shows a female about to lay an egg on a frond of willow moss.

**Fire salamander** *Salamandra s. salamandra.* Common in central Europe, Asia Minor and N Africa, this creature is the originator of the family name. Up to 20 cms in length, it frequents damp places close to water. Delayed births, sometimes occurring as much as two years after pairing, are characteristic of this batrachian. These salamanders are completely terrestrial except during their larval state, when egg-laying and occasionally when the male is fertilizing. They are also nocturnal, spending the day holed-up under stones or dead vegetation. Heavy rain during the day will encourage them to emerge and forage for food. As with many other amphibians, the fire salamander's skin secretes a poison, toxic enough to be fatal to a small mammal but merely irritating to humans. The brilliant yellow or orange markings on the jet black ground are an excellent example of warning colouraion.

TOP LEFT

**The marbled newt** *Triturus m. marmoratus*
is the most beautiful of all European
newts, and the male is particularly
handsome during the breeding season
when he develops a long, black and yellow
striped crest on his back and tail. Unlike
other European newts, *T. marmoratus*
does not sport an orange or red belly but
is more soberly patterned with black and
white markings on a grey background. The
female has a thin, red dorsal stripe and a
warty skin like the male.

ABOVE RIGHT

**The spotted salamander** *Ambystoma
maculatum*. This striking salamander is
found in the same region of Texas and
Nova Scotia as the marbled salamander.
During the springtime breeding season,
large numbers swarm in their favourite
ponds and leave innumerable egg masses in
the water after they have mated. The
gelatinous capsules containing the eggs
often assume a green tinge from their
absorption of algae and sometimes the
larvae perish as the result of the instrusion
of fungus. As soon as they have completed
their metamorphosis, the young
salamanders leave the water and follow
their parents into the seclusion of their
terrestrial retreats.

RIGHT

**The marbled salamander** *Ambystoma
opacum*. Among the least aquatic of its
kind, this North American salamander is
often found considerable distances from
water. Another unusual characteristic is its
breeding season – mating takes place in the
autumn. The female lays 100–200 eggs in
depressions in the ground and then
'broods' them until heavy rains cover the
eggs and promote hatching. In the absence
of rain the hatching remains latent until
the spring. A nocturnal feeder, the marbled
salamander hunts worms and woodlice and
spends the daytime under cover.

LEFT

**The crested newt** *Triturus c. cristatus* is
ubiquitous throughout Europe, east to Centr
Russia and Scandinavia. It is only during
the breeding season that the crest appears
down the male's back and during his
courtship display he continually curls and
flaunts his tail. After mating the female lays
up to 300 eggs and then the pair leave the
water and resume a terrestrial existence until
the following year. While in the water,
their food includes *Daphnia*, mayfly larvae,
mosquito larvae, small fish fry as well as
frog tadpoles. On land they eat slugs,
worms and woodlice.

RIGHT

**The alpine newt** *Triturus alpestris* lives in mountainous regions and is indigenous to France, Spain, Germany, Italy and Greece although it is also found in such low lying countries as Holland and Belgium. They awake from hibernation during the early part of the year and move into the water to mate and lay the eggs which is usually finished by the end of May. During the breeding season the colouring of the male is most spectacular. Neotony is quite common with this species and tadpoles are often found with yellow bodies and red gills.

# Lizards

Lizards of one kind or another can be found in most temperate and tropical regions of the world. In Britain there are two recognizable lizard species, the common or viviparous lizard and the sand lizard. The legless slow worm, which is often mistaken for a snake, is also found in Britain. The more colourful and larger species, such as the green lizard and the eyed lizard, are found in Europe; while the complex representatives of the order Squamata (suborder Saurius) are located in Africa, Asia, Australia and the New World. The Squamata is also shared by the snakes which comprise the second suborder of serpents.

Superficially, the main difference between lizards and snakes is that lizards have legs. However, there are several species of legless lizards, and there are also lizards which possess many of the snake's characteristics so there has to be a more specific anatomical differentiation. Lizards have eyelids and an earhole which snakes don't have; their tongues are notched, not forked and the two halves of their lower jaws are joined together. Lizards vary so much that it is necessary to divide the various species into groups and to treat each group separately.

One of the largest families of lizards is the Iguanidae. Comprising some 700 species, the greater majority of iguanidae are found in the New World. Some iguanas are terrestrial and some adapted for life among the tree branches. Others, like the large marine iguanas of the Galapagos Islands, are almost as much at home in the sea as the sea lions. However, they are herbivorous, feeding upon seaweed. The green iguana, *Iguana iguana*, a beautiful green tree lizard, like a miniature *Iguanadon*, is probably the best known and most often seen in zoos and pet shops.

The Old World equivalents of iguanas are the 300 species of the family Agamidae which are terrestrial, arboreal and aquatic. They range through the Middle East, Indonesia and Australia where the spectacular frilled lizard is found. The frill, in the form of a large neck ruff, is spread to impress anything that threatens an attack.

Geckos belong to a family which contains species indigenous to Asia, southern Africa, South Australia, the southern part of America and New Zealand. They are the only true vocalists of the Saurians, and it is believed that they communicate with each other. Their feet are specially ribbed with bands of tough skin to give them great agility and they are noted for their skill at walking upside down on the ceiling after their prey.

One of the chameleon's characteristics is particularly well known – its ability to camouflage itself almost anywhere by changing its skin colour according to the light conditions. These extraordinary creatures have other characteristics which are not at all typical of the lizard clan. Their eyes move independently of each other and roll around giving them almost total vision. And instead of moving with a lizard's usual lightning rapidity they have perfected the opposite art

ABOVE
**Common lizard** *Lacerta vivipara*. This little lizard has a wide distribution from Europe and Asia to the eastern extremity of Mongolia and as far north as Lapland. It is found throughout the British Isles, including Ireland where it is the only reptile. Like many lizards, *L.vivipara* is able to shed its tail when caught but it can also do so without outside help. This is possible because the tail is waisted at a particular point where the vertebrae is weakened and a rupture can be triggered off by muscular action. Blood vessels taper towards the breaking point and soon heal over with minimal bleeding.

RIGHT
**The eyed lizard** *Lacerta lepida* is the largest European lizard with a length of 60 cms. Of this, the tail accounts for 40 cms. The common name refers to the ocellation of blue 'eyes' along the side of the body. It is a ground dweller but is able to climb trees and will do so when threatened. However, it is often prepared to face the attack and give a good account of itself against a dog or a cat. The bite is harmless but painful. The female lays her eggs in hollow trees or buries them in the ground. Eyed lizards eat a variety of invertebrates, lizards, small mammals, birds' eggs and fruit.

of moving in slow motion and 'freezing' in any position using exceptional muscle control. In contrast, however, they have perhaps the longest, fastest tongues of any lizard. Old World reptiles, the chameleons, inhabit Africa, southern Spain, India, Ceylon, Arabia and Madagascar.

. The more unobtrusive of the Saurians are the skinks of the family Skincidae which contains over 500 species. Mostly of a burrowing disposition and given to a reclusive existence under rocks and plants, they subsist on insects and worms according to the species.

The large lizards are the Monitors comprising the family Voranidae. The largest monitor must be the Komodo Dragon, regarded for many years as a traveller's tale. Reaching a length of more than 3 metres and a weight of 300 pounds (150 kgms), its habitat is restricted to a small group of tiny Indonesian Islands.

Monitors share certain features with the snakes such as a deeply forked tongue and an efficient Jacobson's organ. The gila monster, *Heloderma suspectum*, and the beaded lizard, *H. horridum*, are two venomous New World monitors. Their venom affects the nervous system of the victim, and is shot out from the lower jaw. The Tuatara, *Sphenodon punctatus*, is the sole surviving member of its order and is most closely related to the reptiles whose fossil remains date them as far back as 170 million years, to the mesozoic period. Tuatara is best known for the so-called third eye. Situated on top of the head, this additional 'eye' consists of a crude lens, and is thought to be either a relic of a once functional eye or an entirely different sensory organ which responds to light rays from the sun. It has been found in a more vestigial form among other lizard species.

Many lizards are able to drop their tails if a predator threatens to catch them. The slow worm also has this ability although it is difficult to see where the body ends and the tail begins until the two separate. When the tail does drop off there is quite an audible click like the sound of a snapping wine glass stem. For this reason, *Anguis fragilis* is also known as the glass snake. A detachable tail is a good means of defence since the predator is not unnaturally distracted by the sudden division into two, of its quarry and the lizard has a second in which to escape, leaving the still wriggling tail behind. Naturally. it is reluctant to lose it until actually caught but is able to shed it even if it is only being threatened.

Finally, there are two species of lizards which are quite exceptional: the Basilisk lizard can run on its hind legs like a mammal and the flying dragon from Indonesia can glide up to 40 feet from tree to tree or from a tree to the ground. It does this by extending its special flaps on each side of the body.

# Chameleons and Geckos

**Cape chameleon** *Microsaura ventralis*. This colourful species shows the chameleon's prehensile tail in action and the peculiar grip it employs with its feet. Each foot has five toes, the front feet having three on the inside and the hind ones having three toes on the outside. This unusual arrangement, combined with the chameleon's stealthy air gives him an extraordinary way of walking which is nonetheless efficient for an animal that has to get close enough to its prey to catch it with its tongue. Although the powers of colour change attributed to chameleons have been greatly exaggerated, spectacular variations of pattern and colour intensity are quickly adopted, stimulated mainly by the movement of the sun and the interplay of its light between the foliage.

*Chamaleo lateralis* is a species of chameleon endemic to Madagascar and is found only in the Tananarive area. It has a very complex colour pattern and the photograph exemplifies, in part, the principle by which colour change is effected. The colour cells are in four layers and when the yellow cells, for example, are underlaid by blue ones, the admixture will produce green. Thus the movement of the cells within their respective layers, in response to stimulation by light or by emotion, will produce a wide variety of patterns or, in the extreme, a concentration of one colour. Broken colour patterns usually form in response to the need for camouflage while an overall uniform colour, such as black, serves as a warning to other chameleons.

**Chameleon** *Chamaeleo deremensis*. This species, found only in the Usambaru Mountains of Tanzania, is one of several that have an arrangement of horns on the head. These are larger on the males, but do not appear to serve any useful purpose and are not brought into play during squabbles. Such confrontations are settled by displays of huffing, puffing, change of colour and, on the part of the loser, a fit of the sulks.

**Diurnal gecko** *Phelsuma vinsoni* is a very colourful gecko from Mauritius, and is one of the few exceptions to the large family as it hunts its prey in daylight. It is shown in typical tree-climbing posture and is in search of small insects. The brilliant colouration is possibly for display and for warning off other members of the same species trespassing on its territory. All geckos are oviparous and lay eggs with tough skins requiring long incubation.

BELOW LEFT
**Diurnal gecko** *Phelsuma madagascariensis.* This is another brilliantly coloured gecko which is active during daylight. This close-up photograph shows the large, round pupil and the flattened toes which give the gecko maximum contact for sure footholds. The ear opening is also clearly shown. This species is found in the east coast forests of Madagascar. Completely insectivorous, geckos are very useful to men and those which make their territories inside houses are usually welcomed. The speed and ease with which they run across the ceiling and the skill with which they catch their prey is fascinating to watch.

RIGHT
**Leaf-tailed Gecko** *Uroplatus fimbriatus.* Madagascar has twelve genera of geckos and of these seven are found nowhere else. One such endemic species is shown here. The tail is flattened and the legs and body have a fringe of hair. The colouring affords excellent camouflage among the lichen growing on the tree trunks. It has vertical pupils to its eyes like all nocturnal geckos. Although this gecko might seem to be precariously balanced, the underside of its toes have flaps of skin and tiny hooks so that a very firm foothold is assured on all but the most smoothly polished surfaces.

BELOW
**Web-footed gecko** *Palmatogecko rangei.* Many geckos live in deserts, and this comes from the Namib Desert of southwest Africa. Living in burrows it makes in the sand, it emerges to trap prey such as insects and other invertebrates. For easy movement on the soft sand, it has specially adapted webbed feet. The photograph illustrates this feature and also shows a similar modification of the feet of the insect which the gecko has just caught.

# Agamids

ABOVE
**Frilled lizard** *Chlamydosaurus kingii*. The lizard's frill is of skin stretched over a number of radiating ribs and is normally carried in a relaxed position draped over the shoulders. The lizard's first impulse, when disturbed, is to run rapidly away on its hind legs but if a confrontation is unavoidable, it quickly raises the frill, opens its mouth wide and hisses. Mainly feeding on insects, especially ants, it also consumes spiders and small mammals. The colouring of specimens varies from one region to another, and they can grow to a length of just short of one metre. The lizard in this illustration was photographed in Queensland.

TOP RIGHT
**Arabian toad-headed agamid** *Phrynocephalus* species. These small lizards have flattened bodies which help them rapidly to disappear by wriggling under the sand in a speedy side-to-side movement. They are burrowers, and they have scaly projections over the eyes for protection against falling sand. Their eyelids, too, are equipped with a further ridge of scales for combatting wind-blown sand. The photograph shows a specimen in a posture of alarm, photographed just before making itself scarce under the loose sand. Mainly insect feeders, these little lizards also eat fruit, flowers and foliage when they are available in their arid environment.

RIGHT
**Bearded Dragon** *Amphibolurus barbatus*. This Australian agamid is approximately 50 cms in length and is covered with spines all over, particularly around the throat pouch which can be extended until it resembles a beard. This effect is displayed during courtship and when the lizard is confronted by an attacker it also opens its jaws to reveal its brilliant yellow mouth. If it is disturbed while basking, it sometimes changes colour and the uniform brown becomes yellow with orange bands. Like many agamids, the bearded dragon will run on its hind legs, and it is thought that they do this to keep cool.

**Agama atricollis.** These are the most
common reptiles found in West Africa,
belonging to the Agamidae family and
comprising around 50 species. Like many of
the geckos, they are often found around
human settlements where they exploit the
security afforded by the thatched roofs of
the huts. Active throughout the hours of
daylight, they are always visible, searching
for insect prey, and indulging in territorial
squabbles. It is the males which are chiefly
concerned with guarding their territories
and they have a habit of opening wide
their mouths, which are bright orange
inside, in an attempt to intimidate the
trespassers. The species illustrated measures
around 30 cms in length.

**The moloch** *Moloch horridus* is a small
agamid lizard (20 cms long) from Australia.
Although it cannot be called handsome, it
is quite undeserving of its name. Quite
harmless, it is a dedicated ant-eater and
flicks them up with its tongue in a display of
great speed and dexterity. It is covered with
innumerable spines which endow it with a
formidable appearance matching that of the
so-called horned toads (iguanids) of the New
World.

# Iguanas and monitors

LEFT
**Marine iguana** *Amblyrhynchus cristatus.*
The Galapagos Islands are the home of the
two largest iguanas, the terrestial
*Conolophus subscristatus*, and the marine
species pictured here. This iguana is the
only marine lizard and browses on the
algae exposed at low tide on the rocks.
It clings to the rocks, and tears at the
growth with its mouth. These huge lizards
will dive to depths of ten metres to feed on
seaweed on the sea bed and can remain
submerged for fifteen minutes or more.
Unlike most water lovers, they do not
always seek refuge in the sea when disturbed
because of their fear of sharks which come
inshore at high tide.

BELOW
**Galapagos land iguana** *Conolophus
subcristatus.* When Charles Darwin
investigated the Galapagos Islands in 1835,
he found them inundated with these giant
lizards but since human settlements have
arisen their numbers have diminished
alarmingly. The blame for this is laid upon
the domestic animals and in particular
goats, whose grazing reduces the natural
vegetation which affords the young iguanas
protection against hawks, their chief
predators. The land iguana feeds mainly on
*opuntia* cacti and acacia leaves.

PREVIOUS PAGE
**Green iguana** *Iguana iguana*. These
spectacular lizards are only found in the
New World and in Madagascar. Average-
sized specimens of the green iguana are
often seen in zoos but in the wild this
species reaches a length of two metres or
more. Omnivorous, it is fond of fruit,
supplemented with a variety of insects and
other invertebrates. The spikes on the top of
the head and the pouch, which is an erectable
sac, are both for display to a rival in order
to intimidate. Apart from courting bouts
with other males, the green iguana usually
freezes when danger first threatens. It then
moves very rapidly through the branches
and will drop a considerable distance to
ground, landing safely and making off at
high speed. It can shed its tail but it is such
a useful weapon against adversaries that the
iguana only dispenses with it under extreme
duress. When escape is not possible it will

defend itself by inflicting nasty bites and scratches. Its greatest enemy is man since it is a favourite food with the South Americans; often the iguanas are caught and sold live in local markets.

TOP LEFT
**Green Anole** *Anolis carolinensis*. The anolids are the New World tree lizards and comprise the largest genus of the Iguanid family. They are quite unrelated to the Old World Chameleons although they are often wrongly associated with them because of their ability radically to change colour. After dark the green anole assumes a garb of bright green with a pink throat. It changes its colour in response to stimulation from variations in light and temperature. This photograph shows it wearing the day apparel of brown. Males compete with one

another very fiercely in the breeding season, erecting the skin on the throat and biting and shaking one another.

BELOW LEFT
**Nile monitor** *Varanus niloticus*. Monitors are confined to the Old World and this species is one of the largest, reaching a length of up to two metres. At home on land, in water or in trees, it will take prey where it can, relishing frogs, crabs, rats and even putrifying carrion. Regarded as a pest in many areas, it is an inveterate chicken thief. It shares some features with the snakes including a forked tongue and the habit of swallowing whole chunks of its prey, torn from the carcass with its powerful claws. The female rakes off the top of a termite's nest, lays her eggs in the remains and leaves the termites to cover them in their diligent endeavours to repair the nest.

ABOVE
**Sand Goanna or Gould's Monitor** *Varanus gouldi*. The monitors are exclusively Old World lizards (although fossilized remains have been found in North America) and are represented by one genus comprising 21 species. Several of these are found in Australia where they are called Goannas (a corruption of Iguana) and *V. varius,* the lace monitor, is the largest. The incongruous title of monitor is another example of misunderstanding and poor translation. The Arabic name for these lizards is 'waren' which became confused with the German 'warnen' meaning warning. This was later construed as a reference to the activities of a monitor who rebukes his subordinates for misdemeanors.

LEFT

**Giant Zonure** *Cordylus giganteus*. This
lizard is also known as the sungazer because
it loves to bask in the sun whenever possible.
It is the largest, (37 cm.) of the 23 species of
girdle-tailed lizards, so called because their
tails are protected by rings of large spiny
scales. When disturbed, the giant zonure
seeks refuge in crevices between the rocks
from which it is difficult to dislodge because
it can get so well wedged in by its scales and
the spines on its tail make it impossible to
get a grip. When unable to flee, it flattens
itself to the ground, protecting its vulnerable
underparts and strongly resisting attempts
to overturn it. Its food comprises other sun
lovers such as grasshoppers and small
lizards.

TOP RIGHT

**Worm lizard** *Amphisbaena* species. A corrupt
derivation of *amphivena*, meaning coming
both ways, the generic name refers to the
apparent headlessness of this animal. The
illusion is heightened by its habit of waving
its tail in seeming imitation of a snake's
head in threatening posture. Found in
subtropical and tropical regions, the species
illustrated is from the Namib Desert of
Southwest Africa. These strange, legless
lizards spend most of their time
underground, and are often in ants nests,
since they are immune to their bites. They
move in a worm-like manner, contracting
and expanding their body length.

BELOW LEFT

**Stump-tailed skink** *Tiliqua rugosa*. Skinks
belong to a family of lizards which are
mainly terrestrial, many of them burrowing
underground. Although some species have
long legs, the majority possess short legs
and some none at all. Those which burrow
have small eyes protected by transparent
plates and their eardrums are sunken. The
stump-tailed skink looks as if it is armour
plated and it is difficult to tell which end is
which. Moveover, it increases this deception
by moving backward as fast as it does
forwards. The female delivers only two live
young which are each half her own length.
This skink feeds on insects, molluscs and
small lizards but it is also fond of fruit.
Those kept in captivity have shown a liking
for bananas which are absent from their
native Australia.

RIGHT

**The slow worm** *Anguis fragilis*. Due to its
snake-like appearance, this legless lizard is
often killed on sight, which is a pity since
not only is it absolutely harmless but it also
makes a useful contribution to the control
of garden pests such as small slugs – its
staple diet. The young are particularly
attractive having a brassy or coppery
appearance but the colour darkens with age
to a gun-metal shade which is sometimes
relieved with bright blue spots. Old
churchyards are a favourite haunt. Slow
worms hide under the tombstones during
the day and emerge at night in search of
crepuscular prey.

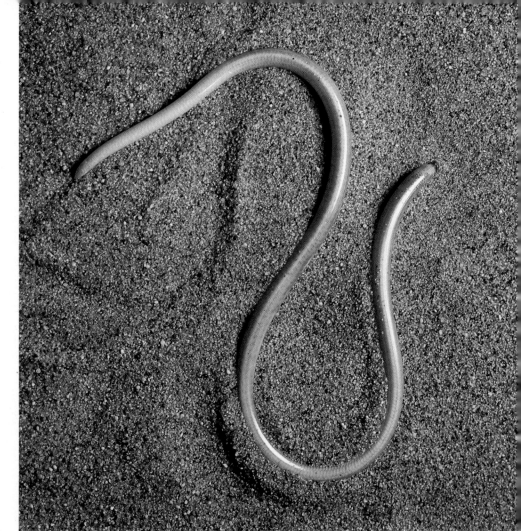

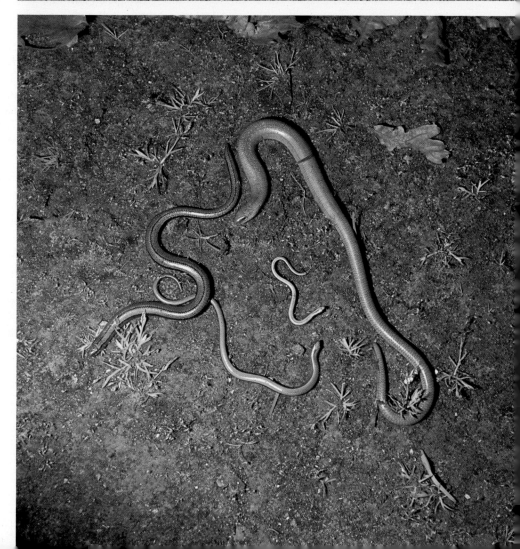

# Turtles and tortoises

The Chelonians comprise the tortoises, terrapins and turtles (commonly lumped together under the heading of turtles in America) and have a heritage going back more than 200 million years. Approximately, 250 species can be found in the tropics with a few scattered throughout more temperate zones. At least four species of turtles are often seen around British coastal waters.

The body is enclosed in a casing consisting of two parts, the carapace or shell and the plastron or base: both have a foundation of bone covered with horny plates or scutes. (The exceptions are the leathery turtle and the so-called soft-shelled turtles.) The vertebrae are mostly fused with the shell while the dorsal ribs are fused with the adjacent bony plates. Breathing within the rigid confines of this box of bone would present certain difficulties were it not for the muscles of the abdomen which contract to allow the creature to inhale. Other muscles exert pressure on the organs near the lungs which are thus squeezed and deflated in the process of exhaling. Some of the turtles and terrapins are able to supplement their respiration when under water by using their cloaca as gills and passing water through it to extract oxygen.

The order Chelonia includes the family Emydidae (the terrapins); the family Testudinidae (the land tortoises); and the family Cheloniidae (the turtles). The most familiar of the Chelonians is the so-called Greek tortoise, *Testudo hermanni hermanni*, which is commonly offered for sale in pet shops and which, with care, can remain a family pet for years. The main physical differences among the families of this order are immediately apparent. Tortoises have sturdy, stumpy legs with short claws. The terrapins have more flexible legs with webbed toes and curved claws. The turtles' legs have become highly developed for aquatic life and take the form of efficient paddles.

It is interesting to note the other differences which exist:— the land tortoises, for example, are renowned for their slowness and proceed at little more than a fraction of a mile per hour while some of the turtles can move at speeds of 15 knots. Most of the terrestrial species are vegetarian but the terrapins and turtles are omnivorous and prefer meat. The snapper turtle of America is particularly voracious and has the reputation of snapping at anything, including wild fowl.

The Hawksbill Turtle, *Eretmochelys imbricata*, was once prized for its shell which supplied the tortoiseshell used in the manufacture of spectacle frames and ladies' fans. The green turtle, *Chelonia mydas*, provides the traditional soup for banquets and this, plus the wholesale collecting of its eggs, has resulted in its extinction in many of its former haunts.

*Lapidochelys olivacea*, a turtle from South American coastal waters is noted for the way it sheds tears after the arduous task of labouring up the beach to deposit its eggs. The tears are produced for the practical purpose of rinsing sand from the eyes and not as an expression of exasperation or sorrow.

It may come as a surprise to many to learn that it is a Chelonian that tips the scales as the heaviest of all the reptiles. The leathery turtle or Luth, *Dermochelys coriacea*, is known to have reached a weight of more than half a ton (just under half a tonne) which is considerably heavier than any of the Crocodilians.

The largest Chelonians, often seen in zoos, are those from the Galapagos Islands which weigh up to 600 pounds (300 kgs). Over a dozen species of giant tortoises once populated the Galapagos Islands but foraging sailors were responsible for their diminution to extinction level. The tortoises from the islands of the Seychelles and Aldabra, once abundant but now thinly represented, also reach giant proportions.

As members of the oldest order of reptiles, the Chelonians have achieved a remarkable degree of protection from predators and this is especially so with land tortoises. When danger threatens, they withdraw their heads totally and the forelegs follow, completely blocking the space between the shell and the base. The hind limbs are similarly retracted and the attacker is presented with a fortress of bone with hard scaley front and rear doors. Excluding grass fires and the occasional intelligent bird of prey, which is said to carry them aloft and drop them on the rocks below to crack their shells, tortoises enjoy a high rate of survival in the wild and sustain more losses in transportation for commercial marketing.

Breeding patterns among the Chelonians do not show any spectacular diversities. Land tortoises deposit their eggs in the soil and leave them to incubate in the warmth of the sun. Similarly, terrapins lay their eggs in damp soil near the water. Turtles, unfitted for really efficient terrestrial activity, struggle up the beach at night and lay their eggs in the sand above the tide-line.

Most of the Chelonians conform to the pattern of their particular family. One or two oddities, though, are found within the family Trionchidae, the soft-shelled turtles, and the sub-order, Plenodira, which includes the snake-necked and side-necked turtles. The soft-shelled turtles have no horny plates and the shell is covered instead with soft skin. Well adapted for an aquatic existence, about two dozen species are found in Africa, Asia and North America.

The snake-necked and side-necked turtles of the southern hemisphere hail from South America, Africa and Australia. When withdrawn, the head is turned aside to lie between the shell and the base at right angles to the body length. The one with the longest neck is Cope's Terrapin, *Hydromedusa tectifera*, which comes from Brazil, Argentina and Uruguay.

# Tortoises

ABOVE
**African hinge backed tortoise** *Kinixys erosa*.
The shell base of this species is not only
hinged so that soft ends close, but also pro-
jects in front so that it can be used for
butting an opponent or rival during mating.
The projection can also be used for over-
turning an adversary so that he is powerless
to rejoin the contest. The photograph shows
the projection just beneath the head and
also illustrates the rich colour and patterning of the shell.

RIGHT
**Leopard tortoise** *Testudo paradalis*. This
attractive tortoise is found in the tropics and
South Africa and has a markedly domed
shell, blotched and spotted with black
markings. The photograph shows one
proving his vegetarian preferences by
champing chunks from a succulent cactus.

**Giant tortoise** *Testudo gigantea*. This species, from the Seychelles Islands in the Indian Ocean, is known to have reached a length of nearly 1.25 metres. An authenticated record exists of a specimen taken to Mauritius as an adult in 1766 which lived until 1918 when it was more than one hundred and fifty years old. Its shell can be seen in the British Museum.

**Giant tortoise** *Testudo elephantopus*. This is one of several forms found in the Galapagos group of islands. While it is believed that each island has a species of its own, the whole are usually classified together under T.elephantopus. Visitors to the islands in the seventeenth century were astonished at the great number of these huge creatures. Their numbers have been greatly reduced since then and it has been necessary to protect them by law. In addition to depredation caused directly by man, domestic animals brought to the islands by colonizers have wrought havoc among the eggs and the young tortoise hatchlings.

**Florida box tortoise** *Terrapene carolina bauri*. This very handsome tortoise is so called because the efficient hinged plastron can completely close the shell to form an almost air-tight box. It is not a strict vegetarian, as the photograph shows. While it enjoys berries and fungi, it also relishes worms, slugs and snails. A remarkable feature of this species concerns the mating when the male assumes, anthropomorphically speaking, a sitting position. During June and July, the female lays her eggs in carefully prepared holes which are then filled in and covered over. The young either emerge during that autumn or hibernate immediately after hatching, eventually appearing the following spring.

# Turtles

BELOW

**The spiny, soft-shelled turtle** *Trionyx spinifer* is a widespread species of North America and has soft, spine-like tubercles around the front of the shell. It can reach a length of 40 cms. The photograph shows a young specimen with attractive markings which become less marked with age. For aquatic creatures they display considerable agility on land. Youngsters run with bodies held well clear of the ground. Insects and crustaceans from the major part of its diet. The pointed snout is a family characteristic, as are the webbed and paddle-like hind feet which have long fourth and fifth toes lacking claws.

TOP RIGHT

**Wood turtle** *Clemmys insculpta*. Aptly named, the wood turtle is usually found near woodland streams. It does travel away from water in search of its food, mainly vegetation. The tail is very long in young specimens, nearly equal to the body length. Its distinguishing feature is its red neck. It is attributed a high I.Q. for it can equal the rat's ability in negotiating a maze.

BELOW RIGHT

**Chicken turtle** *Deirochelys reticularia*. The reticulated pattern of thin lines on the shell is responsible for this terrapin's specific name The base is completely yellow. It is a North American species, and little has been reported about its activities. It is known to frequent secluded waters although remains of road casualities are often found some distances from likely habitats.

# Terrapins

ABOVE

**Diamond-backed terrapin** *Malaclemys terrapin*. This is an estuarine terrapin and is rarely found far from brackish waters. Its popular name derives from the crusty patterning of the shell. These terrapins were once considered delicious to eat and fetched such high prices that they were thought by some to justify controlled cultivation. However, inspite of the great demand, there was no scarcity of wild terrapins. It is unique among terrapins in the marked difference in size between the sexes, adult females measuring 20 cms in shell length against the male's 15 cms. The illustration shows one of these shy terrapins photographed in its habitat.

RIGHT

**Blanding's terrapin** *Emys blandingi*. This terrapin is found mainly in the Greak Lakes of North America and is the only species of the *Emys* genera in America. During the development of the young, a hinge forms in the base which enables the adults to close the front and rear openings between base and shell. The shell is dark brown in colour and carries distinctive markings of yellow speckles. As with most terrapins, the Blanding's diet is carnivorous although they do eat vegetable matter. It is curious that this genus has only two species which are each indigenous to widely separated continents.

FOLLOWING PAGE

**Red-eared terrapin** *Pseudemys scripta*. This colourful little terrapin gets its common name from the scarlet markings behind the eyes. Although aquatic, it spends the hottest part of the day basking on floating logs or on the pond's bank in order to maintain its body temperature. Its food comprises a wide range of aquatic life including small fishes, insect larvae, molluscs and crustaceans. The female lays her eggs in the pondside mud and they hatch towards the end of autumn. The hatchlings have a supply of yolk on which they feed during hibernation.

**European terrapin** *Emys obicularis*. This is
the only congenor of *Emys blandingi* from
North America and is found throughout
Europe and western Asia. Its two-part shell
base is fairly flexible although not enough
to close up the openings each end, as in the
hinged-back species. The tail in young
specimens is as long as the shell but this
proportion reduces with age until the tail is
only half as long as the shell. When emerging from the egg, the young hatchling makes
a hole in the shell with each of its front feet,
breaking away the remaining shell with the
egg-tooth.

**The Caspian terrapin** *Clemmys caspica* is an
attractive terrapin from Syria, Asia Minor
and the Caspian Sea area, usually about 20
cms in length. The shell is not markedly
domed and it is firmly joined to the single-
section plastron or base. There are five
claws on each front leg and four on the hind
legs. All the toes are webbed up to the
claws. Its food comprises small fish, frogs
and tadpoles. It favours ponds and marshes
but is often found far from water and is
capable of rapid movement on land.

# Snakes

It is snakes more than any other reptiles that cause the greatest revulsion and fear in most people. They are also surrounded by the most fanciful stories of evil and magic. Their limblessness and rhythmic movements, the flickering forked tongue and angry hiss seem calculated to produce a reaction of fear and terror. And, of course, the deadly bite that some snakes can inflict has led to the general misassumption that all snakes are dangerous. Yet, this feeling is often tinged with a fascination akin to hypnosis. In some, the fascination leads to a genuine regard for snakes while in others it merely increases the desire to kill. Many of the world's 3,000 or so species of snakes serve a variety of useful purposes; they have an ecological niche in the overall pattern of life, providing food for some animals while exercising control over others. Numerous rodent pests are preyed upon by snakes and the venom from some poisonous snakes has proved of great benefit in medicine as, for example, in blood coagulants.

Before considering the real dangers of some snakes, it is first necessary to dispel some of the widely believed myths. The forked tongue is not the sting weapon but provides the snake with a sense of smell. It is attached to a complex system known as the Jacobson's organ, and enables the snake to follow the trail of prey or of another snake.

Dramatic pictures of trees dripping with hideous snakes ready to drop upon passing humans, pump them full of venom and then constrict them are quite fictitious. Snakes do not attack prey, (other than for food) without provocation and no snake has the means both to inject venom and to constrict. These are quite separate methods of dealing with prey and each is confined to specific types of snakes. The constrictors (boas and pythons) are not as large as popular belief makes out and even the largest of them all, the reticulated python of southeast Asia, is incapable of swallowing prey larger than a small pig. The dislike of snakes is so widespread that even in the most civilized countries these and many more erroneous beliefs abound. In Britain for instance, there are three species of snakes only one of which, the adder or viper, is venomous. Yet, grass snakes and smooth snakes are killed on sight by many people who mistakenly regard them as poisonous. It is still widely believed that a female adder will swallow her young to protect them from danger, regurgitating them when the threat has passed, and that a snake killed during the day will not expire until sundown.

Snakes are divided into 10 families of which the largest, the Colubridae, contains some 2,000 species found in the Old and New Worlds. In the main they are not venomous. Those that are poisonous are known as backfangs because, as well as having solid teeth in both upper and lower jaws, they have one or more fangs in the upper jaw positioned at the rear of the jaw and which are grooved for conducting venom from the venom gland when the bite is executed. Because of the position of the fangs the snake has to perform a chewing action to make them function. Backfangs produce venom that is com-

paratively mild in toxicity.

The South African boomslang (Afrikaans for tree snake) is more dangerous because it strikes with a wide open mouth resulting in instant penetration of the fangs. The venom in all cases is neurotoxic, which means it acts upon the nervous system of the victim.

The subfamily Elapidae comprises many of the more venomous snakes such as the cobras and mambas. These snakes have very efficient grooved or hollow fangs situated nearer the front of the upper jaw and almost under the eyes in which position they are capable of easy and deep penetration. There are about 150 species which are found in America, Australia, Africa and India. Another subfamily of the Colubridae, the Dipsadinae, are nocturnal and prey upon slugs and snails. They are equipped with special jaws; the lower one is used to remove snails from their shells. Members of the subfamily Dasypeltinae prey upon birds' eggs. They pick up the eggs, press down on the shell with the upper jaw to break it and then spit out the broken bits before eating the egg.

Sea snakes, Hydrophiliidae, live permanently in the sea, frequenting areas of the Persian Gulf and regions around Japan and Australia. Their bodies have undergone changes to enable them to swim at speeds comparable with those of the fish upon which they prey, and they have developed special nasal valves to prevent water interfering with their breathing. Since they are venomous, there have been fatalities among fishermen who have caught them in their nets by mistake.

The vipers, viperidae, are the most highly evolved of all the snakes. They possess very large and efficient hollow fangs which are located right at the front of the upper jaw and which can be folded back when not in use. The venom is haemotoxic, acting upon the blood. Pit vipers, including the rattlesnakes and bushmasters of the New World, are members of the family Crotalidae.

The common puff adder is so called because it gives a loud hiss immediately before striking. It is the most common of poisonous snakes in Africa. The puff adder is probably responsible for more snake-bite cases than any other indigenous species because it does not flee when disturbed. It moves in the same way as a caterpillar and is often portrayed by cartoonists unversed in the ways of most serpents.

It may seem, upon cursory inspection, that snakes are a lower order than lizards. They are in fact superior, because although they have lost their limbs, which may seem retrogressive, they have developed a number of faculties which put them in a later and therefore a higher position than the lizards, in the order of developing priorities. Snakes' eyes are lidless but have a transparent covering termed the *brille* which serves instead to protect them. When periodic casting of the skin (sloughing) occurs, the brille is discarded along with the epidermis and a replacement is formed with the new skin. The

more primitive species of snakes have two lungs while the more advanced have a vestigial left lung and use only the right one. The glottis, at the end of the trachea, can be pushed forward out of the mouth so that the snake can breath while it is swallowing its prey. A long gullet, which is large enough to contain any sizable prey that takes time to swallow, leads to the stomach in which digestion is very rapid. Snakes can do without food for long periods and python species have been known to support life for more than two years without feeding. Snakes have no ears nor ear drums and are unable to receive sound. It is generally supposed that they are sensitive only to vibrations. The 'dancing' cobra, no doubt, responds to the vibrations of the snake charmer's pipe, not the sounds which these produce.

# Colubrines

PREVIOUS PAGE, ABOVE
**Garter snake** *Thamnophis species*. Garter snakes belong to a group that divide their time between land and water. Many of them are very aquatic in their habits. These viviparous colubrines are quite harmless and are favourite pets of American children, just as grass snakes (*Natrix natrix*) are of some British schoolboys. Garter snakes are widespread throughout the United States and Canada and live on a variety of creatures from earthworms and frogs to small mammals.

PREVIOUS PAGE, BELOW
**Grass snake** *Natrix natrix*. This is also known as the ringed snake because of its yellow neck band. However, as on this one in the photograph it is not always present. Quite harmless, its only defence is the emission of a noxious fluid from the vent. The grass snake eat frogs almost exclusively, although it has been known also to consume newts and small fish – such variations in diet would appear to differ from one specimen to another. In Britain the grass snake reaches a length of 110 cms but in southern Europe specimens measuring 2 metres have been recorded.

TOP LEFT
**Smooth snake** *Coronella a. austriaca*. This European species ranges north to Scandinavia, south to Spain and eastwards to the Caucasus, and is also indigenous to Britain (except Ireland) although it is becoming rare. Reaching a length of 75 cms when fully grown, the young are born live, breaking from the egg on birth. Frequenting heathland and sandy localities, it feeds principally on lizards and slow worms but is reported to consume nestling birds and small mammals. As its habitat is similar to that of the adder, with which it is often confused, it is often killed on sight although non-venomous and perfectly harmless.

BELOW LEFT
**Corn snake** *Elaphe guttata*. This genus of snakes falls somewhere between those groups which are terrestrial and those which are tree-dwellers. The ventral scales are slightly keeled to obtain a better leverage when the snake climbs the trunk of a tree. *Elaphe* species prey upon terrestial creatures, such as mice and other small mammals, but also climb trees to rob nests of eggs and young birds. The corn snake is non-venomous and relies upon constriction to kill its prey.

ABOVE

**Cross-marked grass snake** *Psammophis crucifer*. This is one of the back-fanged sand snakes abundant in many regions of Africa. Their long bodies enable them to move very fast over the ground after their prey which consists of other snakes, lizards, small mammals and birds. Their enlarged teeth and big poison fangs are typical of the colubrid subfamily Boiginae.

TOP RIGHT

**The hissing sand snake** *Psammophis s. sibilans* is not renowned for its hissing, in spite of its name. This large snake from South Africa reaches a length of 1.8 metres and is one of the commonest snakes in tropical Africa. It feeds on small mammals and lizards and is preyed upon by cobras and predatory birds. Venomous, its bite can cause great pain but is seldom fatal. The young emerge from the 4 cms long eggs approximately 25 cms in length. The photograph shows a hatchling just breaking out of the egg, using its egg-tooth. This is then discarded.

CENTRE RIGHT

**Boomslang** *Dispholiaus typhus*. This is the only rear-fanged snake which is really dangerous to humans because the wide gape facilitates deep penetration by the fangs. It is an arboreal species and, as illustrated, likes to bask on branches but is not a frequenter of thickly-wooden terrain, preferring bush country. Preying on chameleons, tree lizards and young birds, it is unlikely to attack if left alone. Because of its arboreal nature, size and colouring, it is often confused with the mambas though the head is shorter and the eyes larger.

BOTTOM RIGHT

**Common egg-eating snake** *Dasypeltis scabra*. Shown here robbing the nest of a bulbul, this snake comes from tropical and southern Africa. Along with other species, it has become specially modified to subsist on a diet of birds' eggs. Some of the vertebrae in the neck protrude into the gullet to form a structure resembling teeth which serve to crush the eggs. Although the head and neck are no longer than in the grass snake, the elasticity of the egg-eating snake's jaw ligaments is such that it can crush a chicken's egg. It is quite harmless, and relies for defence upon a loud hissing sound made by its erratic coiling and uncoiling which rasps the scales together.

# Vipers and pit vipers

ABOVE LEFT
**Adder** *Vipera berus*. This is Britain's only venomous snake and is common throughout the United Kingdom except in Ireland. It is also widespread in Europe and China. The bite is painful in the region of the wound but is rarely fatal to humans as the adder injects insufficient venom. Small children can be more vulnerable. Adders do not attack, however, unless they really have to, and usually bite only if they have been trodden on or touched by mistake by someone sitting on the ground. They are well camouflaged and are often hard to see when they are sunbathing. Maximum length is around 80 cms and any snake in Britain greatly exceeding this length is likely to be a grass snake. In the illustration, one of the adder's darker colouring is caused by an abnormal development of black pigment in the skin.

LEFT
**Desert side-winding adder** *Bitis peringuey*. A congenor of the horned adder, this species is interesting because of the side-winding gait after which it is named. A small snake of less than 30 cms in length, this adder lives among desert surroundings and its strange style of locomotion is very effective upon loose stones and sand. By flexing its body, it makes a series of lateral movements,

each executed with the body clear of the
ground. The actual motion is difficult to
observe and describe but can be envisaged,
perhaps, from the tell-tale trail comprising a
series of parallel, almost straight, indenta-
tions in the sand. The photograph was taken
in the Namib desert.

ABOVE

**Diamond-back rattlesnake** *Crotalus spp.*
Rattlesnakes belong to a group called pit
vipers because of a small hollow on each
side of the head. This pit is part of a
sensory system, (including the forked
tongue) which enables its owner to detect
warm-blooded creatures in the immediate
vicinity. The rattle comes from a number
of hardened segments at the end of
the tail which, when agitated, produce a
whirring noise, like the sound of dry bones
being rattled together at high speed. There
are several theories concerning the purpose
of the rattle but the most acceptable is that
it is a warning device.

RIGHT

**Gaboon viper** *Bitis gabonica gabonica.* This is
the largest and most attractively patterned
of the African adders and reaches a length
of 1.5 metres. It is a rain forest snake of
sluggish disposition although it can strike
with great speed. Large specimens may
measure as much as 12 cms across the head
and have fangs 5 cms in length. The deep
penetration of such fangs, coupled with the
large amount of venom injected, can result
in serious injury.

# Cobras

BELOW
**Egyptian cobra** *Naja haja*. This is the snake of Egyptian mythology and is best known for its connection with Cleopatra as the 'asp' which put an end to her tumultuous reign. Cleopatra's asp must have been a small one; this picture shows one six feet in length. The venom takes effect quickly and is usually fatal. It lives on toads, small mammals and lizards as well as other snakes but will attack humans if provoked, spreading its hood and presenting a most forbidding spectacle. Conservative in its choice of a home, it will occupy the same hole or retreat for many seasons, always returning after hunting expeditions and when the breeding period is over.

RIGHT
**Indian Cobra** *Naja naja*. This is the familiar swaying occupant of the snake-charmer's basket and the subject of more lurid tales than any other serpent. Factually, no more than ten per cent of its human victims succumb to its venom which is, nonetheless, very toxic. Although it is said to attack without provocation, it does in fact give ample warning of aggression by rearing up and spreading its hood. However, the reputation probably comes from the occasions someone steps on it at night and it is too dark and consequently too late to be warned. The hood is composed of loose skin around the neck which is stretched by the action of the ribs.

TOP CENTRE
**The black-necked spitting cobra** *Naja nigricollis* is one of the most common and dangerous of South African snakes and, like the rinkals, has perfected a method of 'spitting' or ejecting its venom directly into the eyes of its victim, sometimes covering a distance of two metres. While it is able to inflict a fatal bite, it is usually reluctant to do so, preferring to feign death or resort to its spitting technique. It is nocturnal although young specimens are commonly seen during the day.

RIGHT
**Green mamba** *Dendroaspis angusticeps*. This beautiful snake is entirely arboreal and preys exclusively on birds and their eggs. It is only approximately half the length of the black mamba, and it is far less aggressive, since the fangs are incapable of such deep penetration and the venom is less toxic. A fast mover, it has been credited with striking a bird on the wing. Sometimes confused with the green boomslang, it can be distinguished at close range by its smaller eyes and streamlined head. Pairing usually takes place among the tree branches and the eggs are laid in hollow tree trunks or among the fallen leaves.

TOP AND BOTTOM, FAR RIGHT
**The black mamba** *Dendroaspis polylepis* is the largest of Africa's poisonous snakes and reaches a length of 4 metres. It is in fact never black, but a dark, olive green with light underparts. The photograph shows a large, mature specimen draped across a tree, although black mambas are as often found on the ground where they make their home among the rocks or in deserted animal holes. This snake, although notoriously dangerous, is unlikely to attack unless provoked. It does not retreat when disturbed but assumes a defensive posture. With head high above the ground and the gape fully open, it prepares to make a lightning strike accompanied by an injection of venom sufficient to kill five men

# Constrictors

ABOVE
**Anaconda** *Eunectes murinus*. This is the
largest of the boas and comes from northern
South America. It is often believed to
reach a length of 10 metres although
nothing in excess of 7.5 metres has been
authenticated. A river snake, common to
the Orinoco and the Amazon, it
nevertheless feeds mainly on terrestrial
creatures, principally mammals and birds.
It will also eat small crocodiles and
alligators at times. Born live, the young are
approximately 67 cms long. Litters may
contain as many as 30 young.

TOP RIGHT
**Emerald tree boa** *Boa canina*. This arboreal
constrictor is well suited to life among the
branches for its beautiful colouration simul-
ates the foliage and the play of light between
leaves. The photograph illustrates how this
snake manages to rest on a slender, upright
stem: it divides its coils to counter-balance
one another while obtaining its main 'foothold' through the use of the prehensile tail.
Its jaws are well endowed with sharp teeth
for securing its avian prey but it is, of
course, non-venomous.

RIGHT
**Royal or ball python** *Python regius*. Pythons
are the Old World equivalent of the boas
and rely upon constriction for capturing
their prey. Unlike the live-bearing boas,
pythons lay eggs. Both pythons and boas
have vestigial hind legs in the form of claws
beside the vent. This constricted rat was
first knocked senseless by a powerful blow
from the python's head. The large jaws
are equipped with an array of very sharp,
incurving teeth which can cause lacerations.
The lips have sensory pits to assist the
snake's sense of smell when searching for
mammalian prey. Eggs are incubated by the
female who does this by containing them
within her coils.

BELOW RIGHT
**Rainbow boa constrictor** *Epicrates cenchris*.
The most attractive features of boas are
their colour, patterns and the glinting sheen
reflected from the skin. The rainbow boa is
consequently well-named. It comes from
Central and South America while the re-
mainder of the genus is found in the West
Indies. It is equally at home on the ground
as in the trees, dividing its time between the
two habitats.

TOP FAR RIGHT
**Boa constrictor** *Constrictor constrictor*. This
is the New World counterpart of the Old
World pythons although they differ in
several ways. The pythons lay eggs, whereas
the boas produce living young. The boas
also lack part of the upper skull structure
(supraorbital bone). The boas comprise
around 12 genera, and the best
known species is *C. constrictor* which is
found throughout tropical South America
and reaches an average length of just over 4
metres. Boas and pythons have a vestigial
pelvis which contains the same number of
bones as a lizard's pelvis although they have
no union with the backbone. Only the
constrictors possess this evident link with
limb-bearing forbears.

# Crocodiles and alligators

Three families make up the Crocodilian order of reptiles: the Alligatoridae, the Crocodylidae and the Garialidae which has but one species, the Indian Gavial. The Alligatoridae contains two species of alligators and seven caimans while the Crocodilidae has sixteen crocodiles. Members of the three families are scattered throughout West Africa, India, Southeast Asia, China, the Amazon Basin, Australia, Philippines and Central America.

More similarities than differences exist between the three families. Lengths vary from one and a half to seven metres between species. Scaling and head structure constitute the main differences. Alligators, the name derived from the Spanish el larguto, meaning lizard, have broader snouts than crocodiles and the fourth teeth in the lower jaw fit neatly into cavities in the upper jaw; the corresponding teeth in crocodiles remain outside the upper jaw when the jaws are closed. *Alligator mississipiensis* is a less active animal than most Old World Crocodilians and its relative harmlessness may be attributed to its lethargy. The other Alligator, which is found in China, only reaches a length of under one and a half metres and has unwebbed toes.

Mating, which takes place in the water, is a noisy and boisterous affair with savage fights breaking out when rivalry occurs between males. The tough-shelled eggs are either laid in holes dug in the sand or, as with the American Alligator, in a large nest constructed of vegetation and mud. The growth rate of youngsters is rapid.

True amphibians, dividing their time equally between bathing and basking, Crocodilians congregate in groups on river banks and beside lakes and swamps. They are fast swimmers and swift runners on land over short distances. When under water, an arrangement of valves ensures that the breathing system functions while the mouth is open. The ears, too, are protected in this situation by flaps which can be opened and closed as required. The jaws are powerful and amply endowed with strong teeth; the total assembly is a formidable apparatus for dealing with prey which is seized, dragged beneath the water surface, drowned and efficiently torn to pieces for consumption.

Feeding on a mixed diet of fish, mammals and carrion, Crocodilians still enjoy a reputation of latent savagery which is quickly unleashed upon an unsuspecting or foolhardy human. According to authenticated cases, most attacks upon humans have been levelled when they have been in boats or canoes. It could be surmised that the boat, rather than its passenger, presented a threat to the reptile since in some cases, the boat, which was abandoned by the occupants, continued to bear the brunt of attack.

Adult Crocodilians have few enemies other than Man although monitors and herons prey upon the eggs and young. Alligators and crocodiles are slaughtered in great numbers for the soft skin of their underbellies which is much favoured by the leather trade. The caimans are spared this depredation because of the bony plates which cover their underside.

Crocodiles spend the dry season in a state of torpor and dig pits in the mud to keep themselves damp. They spend a lot of time floating entirely submerged with just the eyes and nostrils above the water surface. They achieve this sub-surface floating by swallowing stones which lie in the stomach and serve as ballast to counteract the buoyancy provided by the lungs. Fossilized remains of prehistoric Crocodilians have included a group of stones lying in the stomach area.

Crocodilians have been venerated by various races. Muggers, *Crocodylus palustris*, from Southeast Asia, are still regarded as sacred animals by Moslems and Hindus. The Nile crocodile, *C. niloticus*, was once worshipped by the Egyptians and embalmed crocodiles have been discovered on several burial sites. In ancient Egypt, crocodiles were plentiful but they are now no longer indigenous to Egypt.

The American crocodile, *C. acutus*, is a brackish water creature and although it goes down to the sea, it does not undertake the long sea journeys of the Estuarine crocodile, *C. porosus*.

Caimans are represented by six species and vary in length from 120 cms in the case of the Dwarf Caiman, *Paleosuchus palpebrosus*, to $4\frac{1}{2}$ metres, the length of the Black Caiman, *Melanosuchus niger*. The Black Caiman gets its name from its colouring which is very dark compared to the lighter brown of other caimans. The spectacled caiman, *C. sclerops*, has a ridge between the eyes which appears to link the eyesockets like the nose-bridge of spectacles. Caimans are generally more active and agile and display greater speed of movement both on land and in water than the alligators. They also appear more aggressive when confronted, particularly young specimens which hiss loudly, inflate themselves and prance about like some of the intimidating lizards.

RIGHT
**Nile crocodile** *Crocodylus niloticus*. The
photograph shows a hatchling at the
moment of breaking through the egg. It
was taken at the Zululand Crocodile
Rearing Station of the Natal Parks Boards,
South Africa, where these reptiles are bred
for conservation purposes. The eggs are
approximately six cms long. The vertical
pupil of the eye is clearly shown. It is at
this stage in the wild that crocodiles are
most vulnerable and many are killed by
predatory birds and mammals.

BELOW
**American crocodile** *Crocodylus acutus*. This
is a large species and grows to a length of
four metres or more. Found from Florida
to Mexico and Equador, it favours brackish
water and enters the salt water around the
mouths of rivers where it gathers in
numbers. There are mixed reports of its
behaviour; some people state that it is
dangerous to humans and others argue that
its aggressiveness is due to the age and
condition of the specimen.

ABOVE

**The black Caiman** *Melanosuchus niger* is the largest of the caimans, averaging three metres in length and sometimes reaching four and a half metres. Native to the Amazon and Orinoco basins and Guiana, it is the only species of its genus. Due to its large size, it is a threat to larger animals and for this reason is hunted and killed in large numbers. It tracks down its terrestrial prey at night and catches fish during the day since caimans are essentially water creatures. Although closely related to alligators, caimans have a reputation of being more vicious and likely to attack humans.

ABOVE RIGHT

**American alligator** *Alligator mississipiensis.* There are only two species of alligator and this is the solitary New World representative of the genus. The photograph shows the massive head and very broad snout which is characteristic and also illustrates the concealment of the teeth. In contrast, crocodiles reveal some teeth when the jaws are closed. They can grow to a length of $5\frac{1}{2}$ metres and live for up to fifty years. It is suggested that alligators attain greater ages than crocodiles due to their more leisurely mode of life.

RIGHT, ABOVE & BELOW

**The Indian Gavial** *Gavialis gangeticus.* Also known as the gharial which is abundant in the Ganges, Bramaputra and Indus rivers. The long, tapering snout is an adaptation suiting its owner's exclusive diet of fish caught by swift side-swipes of the jaws. The less bulky shape is better equipped for such action. The gavial grows to large sizes and lengths of nearly three metres have been recorded. It is not reputed to attack humans. The second photograph shows a close-up of the slender jaws and their array of teeth.

# Camouflage and protection

Nearly all animals have certain features specifically designed to protect them from their particular enemies. Camouflage colouring is perhaps the most widespread method through all the animal orders and many members of the insect group, for instance, also depend upon mimicry and warning colouration. Reptiles and amphibians have developed a number of other devices to cope with their own circumstances.

Although some reptiles are viviparous, they are predominantly egg-layers and having deposited their eggs, are forced to leave them, albeit sometimes concealed, to the mercy of numerous predators. The common frog, for example, is most exposed in the egg and as a tadpole and has no built-in defences. As a result adult frogs lay many hundreds of eggs at a time. The common toad lays fewer eggs, but they have a greater chance of survival because the skin secretion, present from the egg stage, is repellant to many predators which destroy frog spawn. Apart from irritating and poisonous skin secretions, amphibians have no active defence mechanisms. None of them has a poisonous bite nor any kind of attacking weapon. Survival therefore depends upon concealment by camouflage, or warning colouration or retreat.

Reptiles have more complex mechanisms including camouflage, warning colouration, rapid retreat from danger, intimidation or bluff and actual aggressive defence. The chameleons are often considered the camouflage experts *par excellence*. Whereas most lizards are continuously moving about and ensuring they are well camouflaged whatever the changes in light and conditions, chameleons often lie in wait for their prey and then move slowly and stealthily, so that, unless their colouring changed according to the light, they would be seriously exposed to predators. Lizards also drop their tails, which gives them a much greater chance of escape when they are pursued from behind. The frilled lizard has an intimidating display as a last resort when it is unable to run away.

The venomous snakes would seem to be better equipped than almost anything else, but, as has been stated elsewhere, even the most deadly of venomous snakes is principally concerned with using its venom for killing its prey, although it will use it against any creature theatening serious attack. Of those snakes which have no venom and no active means of defence some resort to mimicry. The harmless Milk snake (*Lampropeltis doliata annulata*), for example, has the brilliant red, yellow and black bands of the venomous Coral snakes. Some hiss and eject an evil smelling fluid. Others pretend to be dead. The Rinkals or spitting cobra is a case in point, although it is in fact a venomous snake and it is thought that it conserves the venom supply for serious emergencies.

Two of the most serious natural threats to survival which amphibians and reptiles face are the dangers of dessication and extreme cold. Drought is particularly dangerous to amphibians, although they can withstand severe reductions in

ABOVE
**Web-footed gecko** *Palmatogecko rangei*
This illustration shows the gecko emerging
from its burrow.

temperature and survive in water under thick ice. Many of them hibernate, either to avoid cold weather or the heat (like crocodiles).

However, the worst threats to the existence of all amphibians and reptiles are all a direct result of human civilization. In spite of the remarkable adaptions they have made over thousands of years, all of them are now suffering from devastating encroachments upon their habitats and the pollution of water in particular. Even the common frog is in danger, and it is up to men deliberately to preserve areas all over the world where conditions are suitable, not only for reptiles but for all animals, including fish and bird life.

RIGHT

**Cape chameleon** *Microsaura ventralis*. This close-up reveals details of the unusual eye which is turreted and has a small pupil. Each eye can move independently of the other and as they are placed on the side of the head the chameleon has virtually all-round vision. He needs it since he relies upon his quick sight and accurately darting tongue to catch his prey. He also relies upon camouflage as he lies hidden and waits for the insects to fly near him or crawls towards those whose own camouflage his keen eyes have penetrated.

BELOW RIGHT

**The Esturine crocodile** *Crocodylus porosus*. This species is reputed to be among the most savage of the crocodiles. It is truly seagoing, and it frequently makes trips between the islands of the Malayan archipelago. It also makes sea voyages of many hundreds of miles and has been reported as far from its home waters as the Cocoa Islands in the Indian Ocean. The distinguishing feature of this crocodile is the lack of occipital scutes, the enlarged plates found at the back of the head in other species. It grows up to a length of six metres.

BELOW

**Rinkals or spitting Cobra** *Hemachatus haemachatus*. Closely related to the true cobras of the genus *Naja*, the rinkals also spread a hood when preparing to attack. The fangs are developed so that the venom is channelled down them in such a way that it can be directed under pressure at the victim's eyes with unerring aim and with such force that it is effective up to a range of two or three metres. The victim suffers from temporary or permanent blindness, depending on the amount of venom injected. The average length of the rinkals is 125 cms. This snake often feigns death and, with mouth agape, gives a realistic impression of lifelessness before resorting to more positive defence action.

**Edible Frog** *Rana esulenta*. In this illustration
the head of the frog is shown in close-up,
against a background of greenery. The
striking markings, which are particularly
noticeable on the head would only provide
camouflage against stony, sandy ground,
and probably act as a successful flash of
warning as the frog leaps away to a predator
planning an attack.

**Rhinoceros Viper** *Bitis nasicornis*. The bright
colouration and bold, bizarre patterning of
this snake would seem to assure its instant
detection among the leaves and debris of
forest floor. In fact, this viper is superbly
camouflaged and merges completely with its
surroundings. This species shares a similar
distribution to that of the gaboon viper but
prefers to be near water. In addition, it is
smaller than the gaboon viper and rarely
reaches a length of more than 120 cms. The
association with rhinoceros stems from the
large, pointed scales on the end of the snout
which the snake can erect.

*Phrynomerus bifasciatus* is one of the six or
so species of one genus of frogs found in
Africa. *P. bifasciatus* has more than its share
of irritant skin secretion which is exuded in
profusion when the frog is handled. The
secretion can produce inflammation in
humans and possible death to other frogs
which may come in contact with it. An
inveterate burrower, it favours termites'
nests which provide food and seclusion
during dry spells. The skin reacts to light
intensity by changing colour dramatically.
Like many other small frogs (less than four
cms in length), it has a very penetrating call
which is high-pitched and carries for long
distances.

# Acknowledgments

The publishers would like to thank the Natural History Photographic Agency for collecting all the photographs and for giving permission, together with Natural Science Photos, to reproduce them in this book:

Baglin  21, 34, 37, 42 bottom
Bannister  5, 16 top, 19, 20, 22 top, bottom left, 23, 30, 32, 36, 40 bottom, 42, 43, 45 bottom, 57 top, bottom centre, 58 bottom, 60 bottom, 61, 62 bottom, 65 top, 68, 69 top, bottom left, 71
Bille  27 bottom, 29
J B Blossom  45, 46 bottom, 48, 51, 52, 53 bottom, 59 bottom, 70 bottom
S Dalton  2–3, 7 top, 10 top, 14 top, 25 bottom, 26 bottom, 28, 53, 55 bottom, 58 top, 70 top
Hans Dossenback, Natural Science Photographs  63 top right, bottom
M Freeman  Natural Science Photographs  62 top, 66 left
A G C Grandison  22 bottom right, 31 bottom
B Hawkes  26 top

D P Healey  35 top
P Johnson  31 top, 33
K B Newman  57 bottom
L Perkins  7 bottom, 8–9, 10 bottom, 12, 13 top, 14 bottom, 24, 25 top, 43 bottom, 56 top
R Perry endpapers  38, 39, 47
G Pizzey  41, 69 bottom right
I Polunin  17
E H Rao  60 top, 67
P Scott  4
T Stack  59 top, 63 top left, 65 bottom, 66 right
Turner  35 bottom
L A Williamson  13 bottom, 46 top
J N Wood Natural Science Photographs  11, 15, 16, 18, 27, 40, 49, 50, 55 top, 56 bottom

Jacket photographs: A Bannister, J B Blossom, Bille, S Dalton

First published in 1974 by
Octopus Books Limited
59 Grosvenor Street, London W1
ISBN 0 7064 0401 7

© 1974 Octopus Books Limited

Distributed in USA by
Crescent Books,
a division of Crown Publishers Inc.,
419 Park Avenue South,
New York, N.Y. 10016

Distributed in Australia by
Rigby Limited
30 North Terrace, Kent Town
Adelaide, South Australia 5067

Produced by Mandarin Publishers
Limited, 14 Westlands Road,
Quarry Bay, Hong Kong

Printed in Hong Kong